MANAGEMENT THOUGHTS IN *THIRUKKURAL*

MANAGEMENT THOUGHTS IN *THIRUKKURAL*

By
K. NAGARAJAN
M.E., M.B.A., C.A.I.I.B., D.F.S., P.G.D.P.M.

ANMOL PUBLICATIONS PVT. LTD.
NEW DELHI • BANGALORE

ANMOL PUBLICATIONS PVT. LTD.

Regd. Office: 4360/4, Ansari Road, Daryaganj,
New Delhi-110002 (India)
Tel.: 23278000, 23261597, 23286875, 23255577
Fax: 91-11-23280289
Email: anmolpub@gmail.com
Visit us at: www.anmolpublications.com

Branch Office: No. 1015, Ist Main Road, BSK IIIrd Stage
IIIrd Phase, IIIrd Block, Bangalore-560 085 (India)
Tel.: 080-41723429 • Fax: 080-26723604
Email: anmolpublicationsbangalore@gmail.com

Management Thoughts in Thirukkural

First Edition, 2002

Reprint, 2011

PRINTED IN INDIA

Printed at Mehra Offset Press, Delhi.

To

My affectionate daughters

Gaayathri and Harine

who

Keep me cheerful

by

Their innocent mischief

CONTENTS

ACKNOWLEDGEMENTS

I am indebted to my school teachers who planted the seed of urge in me to read ancient Tamil literatures. I take this opportunity to acknowledge their guidance and compassion. I will fail in my duty if I don't express my gratitude to Miss Rema C. and Miss Tharani S. who have converted my scribbles into readable material.

PREFACE

Thirukkural, the book of wisdom, is a hallmark of ancient Indian civilization with a rich heritage, tradition and culture. It was written by saint *Thiruvalluvar*, who was born near Chennai in 30 BC. It is a book that has stood the test of time for over 2000 years and still remains relevant as a guiding force for the mankind. The book written in Tamil language has been translated into almost all leading languages of the world.

Thirukkural has been divided into three major divisions, viz., Virtue, Wealth and Love. It has in all 1330 Verses. The Verses are in the form of couples, rich in meaning, rhythm and diction. No area of human life has been left untouched by this great work by the Tamil saint.

In this small book, I have made humble attempt to identify 89 couplets from *Thirukkural* that have in them the essence of management thoughts of the ancient times and I have related the meaning of these couplets to the contemporary management thoughts. Contemporary Management thoughts on the selected topics are explained in brief, interlaced with relevant couplets of *Thirukkural* that contain in them the wisdom of

Thiruvalluvar. The entire work is so revealing that it would benefit both practising managers and students of management studies immensely. One would find in the words of *Thiruvalluvar* a striking coincidence with the contemporary management thoughts and at times the wisdom of *Thiruvalluvar* would stand high above the contempory thinking. I am sure that any reader of this small book will be taken by surprise by the wealth of information available from the tiny couplets of *Thirukkural* and the mode of diction that is crisp and to the point.

There is a general notion that the Contemporary principles of Business Management have mostly evolved from Western thoughts. In fact, there is a lot contributed by Ancient Indian Scholars to this field, which however, lay undisclosed to the benefit of students, scholars, researchers and practising managers.

I am confident that one who has read this book will recognise the richness and advancement of ancient Indian Civilization.

I have only made a small beginning to introduce *Thirukkural* to management students and practising managers and there is much more to learn and realise from the great Book. It is a treasure house from which one can dig out a lot of wealth.

If I could kindle interest in the minds of readers to study *Thirukkural*, the book of All Time, in depth I would be happy that I have done my job.

—K. Nagarajan

ADAPTABILITY

Life is becoming more and more volatile. Change has become a permanent feature. The only thing that is certain is uncertainty. All business enterprises operate in an environment that is subjected to continuous change. Managers must be capable of adapting to changing environment. They must infuse the quality of 'adaptability to change' into their organisations.

Dr. Joseph L. Massie, in his book *Essentials of Management* defines management of change as " a conscious, concerted initiative by those who are in charge of the destiny of the business undertaking to keep a constant and intelligent watch over the behaviour of uncontrollable forces, to assess their impact and influence on the controllable forces and to evolve appropriate strategies and action programme to maintain a dynamic equilibrium between the controllable and uncontrollable forces" - a lengthy, but accurate definition.

All business enterprises are subject to two types of forces. They are the controllable forces and the uncontrollable forces.

Controllable forces are those about which sufficient

information is available. Hence, the management can plan in advance and manage these forces quite easily. The uncontrollable forces are those about which not much is known and about which no accurate prediction can be made. These forces even have their influence on the behaviour of the controllable forces. Some of the uncontrollable factors are changes in population, shifts in consumer preferences, changes in factors of production, changes in social, political conditions, changes in economic trends, changes in technological advancements etc.

An organisation should adapt itself to the changing environment. Failure to adapt to changes will lead the organisation to ruin, for sure.

"Who adopts not, boasts pride and ignorant

he is sure to have a speedy end."

(Verse 474, *Thirukkural*)

Thiruvalluvar gives three different attitudes that organisations may show in response to the changing environment.

The management of the organisation may be aware of the changes taking place in the environment, but may fail to adapt to the changes due to internal constraints. The management may sometimes be even ignorant of the changes taking place in the environment. Sometimes the management may be aware of the changes taking place in the environment, but may choose not to adapt, having false confidence on its past laurels. *Thiruvalluvar* cautions that all these three attitudes are dangerous, when he says the unadaptable, the ignorant and the proud will all have speedy ends.

Any change is likely is to destabilise a person's existing alignment with his environment. Hence, it is normal that employees put up resistance to change. It is the job of the manager to educate the employees about the need for the changes in the organisation inorder to adapt to the changing environment. Employees may have fear that changes might bring about unemployment, demotion etc. They may feel that it would be difficult to learn new methods and techniques and to learn new ideas. They may even feel that changes are introduced only for the benefit of the organisaiton and not for their benefit.

People resist change only because they do not know it well and its real consequences. The manager, as a change agent, is responsible to educate the employees about the need for the change and to introduce the required changes in a suitable and efficient way. When the world around changes, one should adapt to the changing circumstances. Else, he will be left alone or swept away by the sweeping changes.

> *"It is wise to act the way*
>
> *the world acts."*

(Verse 426, *Thirukkural*)

The recent management thinking in terms of 'Business process Re-engineering' is only a step ahead of adapting to changes. Business process Re-engineering is a continuous review and redesigning of business to suit its environment.

Michael Hammer and James Champy in their book *Re-engineering the Corporation* define Business Process Re-engineering as the fundamental rethinking and radical redesign of business processes to achieve dramatic improvements in critical, contemporary measures of performance, such as cost, quality, service and speed."

The words 'fundamental rethinking' emphasises the need to consciously evaluate to see if the organisation is update with its environment, to identify if the functions of the organisation have not become obsolete, inappropriate and irrelevant to the changing conditions. The words 'dramatic improvements' indicate that Re-engineering is not about making marginal or incremental improvements, but about achieving quantum leaps in performance.

The evolution of the concept of Business Process Re-engineering is to make the organisation fit enough to face the ever changing environment and to face the ever growing competition. In other words, an organisation will continue to survive only if suits the requirement of the world and satisfies the world's needs continuously.

"Those who do not act according to the world
are ignorant though learned."

(Verse 140, *Thirukkural*)

ADVICE
(Heeding to Advice)

Most managers tend to take a defensive stand whenever any one offers, or even shows willingness to offer advice. It is as if the process of accepting advice is a process of admitting one's own ignorance and exposing one's inadequacies.

It is also not uncommon to see more assertive managers who develop barriers against advice. Such an attitude will only act as a barrier for effective communication inside the organisation, which in turn will lead to chaos, misunderstanding, misinterpretation and inefficiency.

Managers must accept the fact that one can not be an expert in all fields. In fact, it is not essential that a manager should be an expert in any or every field. He should be one who knows something about everything. Such a person can turn out to be an effective manager, provided he heeds to the advices of experts in specialised functional areas. It needs a lot of will-power, understanding, self-analysis and magnanimity to recognise others' talents. Moreover, managers should realise that there is nothing to lose by heeding to advices. If at all there is any effect of heeding to advices, it is only the betterment of the individual and the organisation.

Managers who resist advices will have a tough time especially when there is an organisation change or when a new boss/chief executive comes in.

Thirukkural advocates one to seek advice from the wise and act after a careful thought. Though a manager is advised to seek advice from the wise (experts in functional areas), it is not expected of a manager to act strictly as per the advice. He is to make a careful analysis of the advices of wise counsels before arriving at a decision and act accordingly.

"Nothing is difficult to those who act

on the advice of the wise, after careful thought."

(Verse 462, *Thirukkural*)

"Learning the intricacies of tasks from experts

is the way to execute such tasks."

(Verse 677, *Thirukkural*)

It is in fact impossible for a manager to gain expertise in all functional areas that exist in the organization. For managing the affairs of the organisation effectively, it is enough if the manager learns the intricacies of the different tasks from the respective functional experts.

AGRICULTURE (Importance of Agriculture)

Agriculture is the backbone of any economy. It is seen from the history that agricultural development always preceded industrial development. Economic development of a country depends upon agricultural development. This is more so in countries like India that is predominantly agricultural in nature in view of the vast agricultural resources available. Agriculture is one of the oldest occupations of people of the world. It still remains the vital sector for any economy. However, agriculture as a career is not preferred by the educated youth since they hold the notion that it has a lower social status. In most of the developed economies of the world, savings from the agricultural sector has flown into non-agricultural sectors like industry, trade & commerce, transport etc. Thus, for the development of non-agricultural sectors, the existence of a strong agricultural sector has always been the prime requirement.

Agricultural and non-agricultural sectors are mutually dependent on each other. The agricultural sector feeds the people in all the sectors of the economy. It also supports industrial sector by providing raw materials for industries.

It supports transport sector by providing opportunity for the transportation of food grains and other agricultural produces, manure, fertiliser etc., Agriculture also supports service sectors like finance and marketing sectors of the economy.

"Farmers are the axle-pin of mankind,
as they support all others who do not till the soil."

(Verse 1032, *Thirukkural*)

If an economy flourishes with industrial activity, a person with insight will know that there exists an agricultural sector in the economy that contributes to the growth of the industrial sector. If industrial sector flourishes in a country without any agricultural sector, it only means that the industrial sector in the country is supported by the agricultural sector in some other country. For instance, an industrial economy like that of Japan can not thrive on its own unless supported by other countries that have grown with the help of agricultural sector.

It is imperative that a manager, whatever be the field of his engagement, must have a clear vision about the part played by the agricultural sector. Business cycle that occurs in all the economics across the world, to a major extent, depends on the performance of agricultural sector. Since agriculture depends on the vagaries of monsoon in most of the countries of the world, the behaviour of business cycle also exhibits unpredictable variations. Hence a manager in industry can not ignore the performance of agricultural sector. Industrial prosperity depends upon agricultural performance.

Agricultural and industrial sectors are complementary to each other and the existence of one sector depends on the existence of the other sector. Considering industrial sector as superior to agricultural sector is folly. Mankind can live without industry, but not without agriculture. Thiruvalluvar who knows the importance of agriculture, declares it as the most esteemed work.

"Howsoever seen, the world depends on farming; thus despite hard to perform, it has the highest regard."

(Verse 1031, *Thirukkural*)

A Manager in industry / trade and commerce must keep vigil over the happenings in the agricultural sector and he should try to establish the correlation between the agricultural and other sectors of the economy which will stand him in good stead in his macro level planning.

ANGER

When there is disagreement of views or conflict, people often experience primary feelings like frustration, hurt, guilt, insecurity embarrassment etc. These primary feelings develop the secondary feelings of anger.

Anger is one of the unfavourable attitudes of a manager. Anger takes control of the person who is angry and distorts his perceptions. This is why, angry people are often found to make poor decisions. Anger affects the mental health of managers and executives. Only mentally healthy people enjoy life. They are self confident, satisfied, good at having cordial relations with others, able to handle problems satisfactorily without being disturbed, not fearful of situations and they follow their conscience in their behavioural pattern. A person who is not keeping good mental health due to his anger is expected to have behavioural patterns exactly opposite to what have been stated above.

Thiruvalluvar's advice is to get rid of anger in any case.

"Forget anger, in any case, towards anyone
Else only evil and pain will be the outcome."

(Verse 303, *Thirukkural*)

Thirukkural views the futility of anger from a new dimension as under.

"It is wrong to be angry against the weak

while it is futile against the powerful."

(Verse 301, *Thirukkural*)

According to *Thirukkrual*, it is unjust to be angry with the weak. One should try to find out some other ways of resolving the conflict with the weak rather than feeling angry with them. Angry against the strong is not going to serve any useful purpose. It may only lead to a wastage of time and effort and destruction of physical and mental well being. Anger spoils the human metabolism and acts as the root cause of many physical and mental ailments. It may even ultimately kill a person.

Buddha said,

"You will not be punished for your anger;

you will be punished by your anger."

Thirukkural speaks in the same voice of Buddha.

"To safeguard oneself, let one keep away from anger

else he will be killed by his own anger."

(Verse 305, *Thirukkural*)

What is the use of anger, when it is unjust against the weak, futile against the strong, when it spoils one's physical and mental health and goes to the extent of even slaying him and when it kills laughter and love ?

Executives are to keep anger at a safe distance if they want to enjoy their life and work.

> *"Is there any enemy more injurious than anger*
>
> *that spoils laughter and happiness ?."*

(Verse 304, *Thirukkural*)

BUSINESS ETHICS

Webster's ninth new collegiate Dictionary defines ethics 'as the discipline dealing with what is good and bad and with moral duty and obligation'. Ethics desired to be followed by a society get formulated in the form of laws. Thus laws are nothing but ethics formalized by a society. Business ethics is concerned with truth and justice practised by business community.

Koontz and Donnell observe that ethical behaviour is just and fair conduct which goes beyond complying with laws and Government regulations. Putting it in simple terms, ethical behaviour is adhering to moral principles. All individuals have a moral obligation to do good to the society. Albert Einstein, the greatest scientist the world has seen, expresses his feelings on his obligations to the society in the following words

"A hundred times every day I remind my self that my inner and outer life are based on the labours of other men, living and dead and that I must exert myself in order to give in the same measure as I have received and am still receiving....."

When a person who has made the greatest contribution to the scientific development of the world feels the necessity obligation and compulsion on his part to serve the society, it is more so with the rest of the individuals.

Business as an entity is equally under obligation to do good to the society as are the individuals, and so it is obligatory on the part of business to tread the path of equity, truth and justice and never do anything that is against the welfare of the society.

Private enterprises are no doubt formed with the objective of earning profit. Survival of an enterprise depends on the profit that it generates. The question that remains to be answered is as to whether it is permitted to earn profit even at the cost of sacrificing social welfare. Morality prohibits such an option. Moral values and good business ethics should always be placed ahead of profit motives. Modern business is yet to reconcile on this issue. Business enterprises consider ethical behaviour as one that requires an assessment of whether or not a decision / action is right to wrong, given the values of society, rather than a determination of whether the decision of action is legal or illegal. *Thiruvalluvar* does not want to compromise on this.

He gives a two line answer to the moral values and ethics to be followed by business in uncompromising and unequivocal terms.

"Even if gainful, keep away at once

from acts that are unjust and devoid of equity."

(Verse 113, *Thirukkural*)

It is due to ignoring moral values and compromising with illegal attitudes, we have today business enterprises that are engaged in producing goods and offering services that have an adverse impact on the welfare of the society. It is also because of this that we come across unfair trade practices and unethical approaches in business.

CAPITAL INVESTMENT DECISIONS

Capital investment decision represents one of the most crucial decisions taken by a firm. This is because of the reason that capital investment decisions have long term effects, the investments once made are irreversible and the investments need substantial outlay of capital.

In the words of wisdom of *Thirukkural*, the actions to be taken before venturing upon an investment decisions are as under.

> *"Weigh the task, strength of foes, allies*
>
> *and your own strength; then launch action."*
>
> (Verse 471, *Thirukkural*)

Thirukkural advises to weigh judiciously the nature of task. The entire gamut of market analysis, technical analysis and economic analysis are contained in it. Apart from studying the nature of task, *Thirukkural* advises to weigh the strength of foes, allies and the organisation's own strength. This is nothing but an environmental analysis which the modern management explains in terms of ETOP/SWOT [Environmental

Threats and Opportunities Profile/Strength, Weakness, Opportunities and Threats] analysis.

Capital investment, in essence, is the present outlay of funds in return for an expected flow of benefits in future. Whether to opt for project 'A' or project 'B' and within a chosen project whether to go in for machine 'A' or machine 'B' etc., are not matters of tossing the coin, but such choices would depend on a careful evaluation of the cost-benefit of the alternatives.

> *"Examine the costs, returns and profits*
> *before venturing upon a project."*
>
> (Verse 461, *Thirukkural*)

It is the excess of benefits over costs that should be the consideration in financial analysis. This point is again stressed by *Thiruvalluvar* as under:

> *"No matter even if income is small*
>
> *as long as expenses do not exceed income."*
>
> (Verse 478, *Thirukkural*)

COMMUNICATION

Communication is an essential element of directing function. The effectiveness of a manager depends on his ability to communicate. Communication is the lifeblood of an organisation and encompasses all activities in the organisation. According to a report of The American Management Association, a supervisor spends at least 90 percent of his working time communicating one way or another.

Louis A. Allen defines communication as under :

> "Communication is the sum of all things one person does when he wants to create understanding in the mind of another. It is a bridge of meaning. It involves a systematic and continuous process of telling, listening and understanding."

Planning, organising, motivation and control can be achieved only through effective communication. Planning of the top management is communicated downward to the employees of the organisation. The tasks and resources assigned of the employees are again communicated by way of downward communication.

Employees are motivated by keeping them informed (i.e., communicated) on matters which concern them.

Employees communicate to their superiors (Upward communication) about their needs and problems and seek solutions. There is also a need for lateral communication to help Co-ordination and building up team spirit.

Failure to inform and failure to understand what others really mean are the causes of endless trouble. Communication does not merely mean sending or receiving of the message. It is much more than that.

It includes proper understanding of the message, its acceptance and action on it. Communication is complete only when the message transmitted by the sender is correctly understood by the receiver. For the receiver to understand the message correctly the sender should be careful enough to communicate in the right sense without any ambiguity and in a way that is best understood by the receiver. A manager should possess good communication skills to give out messages effectively.

Let us see what *Tirukkural* has to say on this.

"Speaking clearly, conveying correct meaning and discerning,

the subtlest meaning hidden in others' words is wisdom."

(Verse 424, *Thirukkural*)

Thiruvalluvar gives two important qualities of a leader. Firstly, the leader must be capable of conveying his views to his subordinates in clear terms, without giving room for misunderstanding or misinterpretation. This requires great skills. Secondly, *Thiruvalluvar* emphasises another important quality of a leader, viz., that of listening and understanding the messages given by others. It is proper to expect a manager to be a good conveyor of messages. However, his subordinates may not be having the required skills to convey their views to the manager in unambiguous terms. They can not be expected to be experts in upward communication. Hence a manager must be an expert to read between the lines and understand what his subordinates really want to convey to him. Thus, to be a good communicator, a manager should have skills to convey his messages effectively and to discern clearly the meaning contained in the messages that he receive from others.

COURTESY

Courtesy means considerate of others in small ways, showing respect for others, and treating everyone, regardless of position with consideration.

"The greater the man, the greater the courtesy."

—Alfred Tennyson

"Kindness along with gentlemanliness constitute courtesy."

(Verse 992, *Thirukkural*)

Courtesy is an essential quality required of a manager. A good manager always gives consideration to every individual he deals with. He listens, considers others' views, recognises their preferences, respects their feelings. He behaves so, since he always puts himself in the other person's shoes and views issues from there. He will never deliberately make another person look or feel small. His presence among his people will not be a mere physical presence, but he will be mentally present with all those around.

The degree to which a manger can identify with the other person's feelings, is the degree of consideration he has. A good manager will be highly compassionate. Kindliness is one of the greatest virtues that a manager should possess to get maximum output from his subordinates with minimum effort.

"Neither in the earth nor in the heaven it is easy to find

a greater virtue than kindness."

(Verse 213, *Thirukkural*)

A courteous manager will always be sweet in his words, with smile on his face. It is hard to find him frowning, aggressive and ruthless.

"Sweet words with a smiling face are even better

than granting gifts with a joyous mind."

(Verse 92, *Thirukkural*)

Courtesy is such an important quality to be possessed by all human beings [leave alone a manager], that *Thiruvalluvar* advises not to be discourteous even with those who are unfriendly.

"It is not good of the wise to be discourteous

even toward the discourteous who do harm."

(Verse 998, *Thirukkural*)

"As ridicule wounds the feelings even in jest

the noble will be courteous even towards foes."

(Verse 995, *Thirukkural*)

A courteous manager will achieve with ease what an uncourteous manager strives hard but fails to achieve. The energy levels of subordinates who work under a courteous manager will remain quite high so that no task will be an uphill task for the organization.

DECISION MAKING

Decisions are taken at every stage, be it in private life or in organisational environment. Every manager makes many decisions in a day's work knowingly or unknowingly. A decision can be defined as 'a course of action consciously chosen from available alternatives for the purpose of desired result' (J.L. Massie). Managerial decision making include taking decisions relating to planning, organising, staffing, directing, coordinating and controlling.

The steps involved in a decision making process are as under.

- Identify the problem
- Analyse the available courses of actions for the problem
- Develop alternative solutions
- Select the best alternative solution
- Implement the decision
- Follow up

The first step is to identify the problem and to find

its root cause. Only if the cause of a problem is spotted accurately, its cure can be effected. If the staff go on a strike, it need not be for a hike in their salary, though this may be one of their demands. Behind their demand for a salary hike, there may lie some other real cause. For arriving at the right decision, the first step is to know the real cause of the problem.

> *"Identify the disease, diagnose its root cause, ascertain*
>
> *the curative remedy and then apply the same."*

(Verse 948, *Thirukkural*)

Though the above verse appears in a chapter relating to medicine for physical ailments, it is equally applicable for any managerial problem. If the root cause of a problem is not identified, the solution to the problem will be elusive.

Any problem will have more than one way of solving it, Comparison of alternative solutions, in terms of consequences attached with each alternatives helps a manager to choose the best suited solution from among the probable solutions.

> *"Achievement is not impossible to those who evaluate possibilities*
>
> *and choose that is possible to achieve."*

(Verse 472, *Thirukkural*)

Once the best suited course of action is selected, the next step is to implement the same without hesitation. Since all pros and cons are taken into account before arriving at the best possible course of action, there is no point in hesitating to implement the decision or to think of having a second look at the problem. The very idea of having a second look at the problem would only mean that the decision at the first instance would not have been taken after due deliberations.

> *"Take up a mission only after careful deliberations;*
>
> *hesitating after commitment will be reproachful."*
>
> (Verse 467, *Thirukkural*)

When a course of action is under implementation, it must be followed up continuously to ensure that it is implemented fully as per the plans, without any delay and without getting struck up mid way.

> *"Strength of mind fulfills an act to perfection; work*
>
> *delayed or exposed midway ends in peril."*
>
> (Verse 663, *Thirukkural*)

EQUITY

It is imperative on the part of a manager to be fair and just in his dealings with his people. He should treat all his subordinates equally. He should go out of his way to ensure that personal prejudices never intrude upon in his decisions and never show up in his conversations. It is a very subtle thing and managers being human beings, are likely to get carried away by personal prejudices, and that too unknowingly. Hence, they should act cautiously and weigh each of their words and actions to ensure that they are fair.

"A manager can be right, a manager can be wrong,

but a manager should never be unfair."

—Dr. David Freemantle

"To act like a balance scale's arm that inclines to neither side

and thus judge impartially is ornament of the wise."

(Verse 118, *Thirukkural*)

Rather than treating others as unique individuals, prejudiced people tend to think in terms of stereotypes.

Stereotypes are generalizations made about all members of a particular group. People holding stereotypes can form prejudiced attitudes towards one group or another person, regardless of other elements that prove the stereotype invalid. Stereotypes are harmful, but it is very difficult to get rid of them. This is because stereotypes are formed during childhood. Children learn attitudes and beliefs from family, friends, and other authority figures, and learn how to view and treat different racial, ethnic, sex, religious, age and other groups. When children become adults, they carry on with them these attitudes and beliefs that they acquired during their childhood, without testing their validity against their own adult experiences. Even when their adult experiences are different, people more readily believe information that confirms their stereotypes than evidences that challenges them. People act in a prejudiced way guided by the stereotypes that they have already formed.

Stereotypes can be both positive as well as negative. When a manager believes that engineers are good at reasoning, it is a positive stereotype. When a manager believes that women are not suitable for strenuous jobs, it is a negative stereotype. Both are equally bad since they are just beliefs and not realities.

"Impartiality that is not influenced

by love, hate or apathy is great."

(Verse 111, *Thirukkural*)

Prejudices can be formed by love (positive

stereotype) or hate (negative stereotype). Thiruvalluvar shows yet another dimension of stereotype - viz., 'apathy'. Prejudices can be formed not only by love or hate but also by indifferent attitudes. When a manager is indifferent to a particular idea, he will fail to notice the favourable / unfavourable attributes hidden behind that idea.

Though it is very difficult to overcome personal prejudices, it is very essentially required of a manger to look critically and honestly at the particular myths and preconceived ideas he is conditioned to believe about others and change his views, if need be.

Thiruvalluvar cautions that if a person fails to take note of this, he is sure to be ruined.

"Let one who prefers not to be impartial

be warned that he is sure to be ruined."

(Verse 116, *Thirukkural*)

FORBEARANCE

An organisation is a kaleidoscope of different personalities. There will be people who commit mistakes, who disagree with their colleagues and subordinates, who disagree even with the boss, who are gossip-mongers, who are negative in their attitudes, who are unable to learn etc., A good manager absorbs the whole range of frustrations and takes action only when performance is threatened. He should have a higher tolerance limit inorder to concentrate on achieving goals rather than shouting back at the crowd.

"It is a great quality to bear with those who scorn us

just as the Earth bears with those who dig into her."

(Verse 151, *Thirukkural*)

A Manager who forbears silly misbehaviours and petty indifferent attitudes of his subordinates must not carry home their impressions and bring them back to office the next day. He must discard such futile issues and concentrate on achievement of goals.

"It is good to bear with reproach;

still better it is to forget it."

(Verse 152, *Thirukkural*)

It is not only the subordinates who will indulge in inappropriate and indifferent activities, but even the peers may act irrationally and unreasonably. At times even the boss may be behaving in an odd manner. A good manager should have the resilience to tolerate such nuisances. If a manager gives importance to such things, he will be only wasting his precious time and effort.

When a subordinate sincerely admits his mistake, an effective manager will tolerate the subordinate's lapses and guide him/her to learn from his/her mistakes. When subordinates disagree with him, the tolerant manager will not get disturbed, but will consider their views and try to see if they are right in differing with his views.

By adopting a tolerant attitude, the manager can win over those who are responsible for causing anguish to him and his forbearance will bring him lasting honour.

"Overcome by forbearance, those who may

harm you by their prideful act."

(Verse 158, *Thirukkural*)

"Revenge might give pleasure for a day;

but forbearance will bring glory for ever."

(Verse 156, *Thirukkural*)

GOAL SETTING

Objectives are open-ended attributes denoting a future state or outcome that an organisation strives for, while goals are closed-ended attributes that are precise and expressed in specific terms. The most common example given in the books on strategic management is that, when a Company wants to increase its market share, it is the objective that the Company strives for, while the goal to reach the objective might be "to raise the existing market share of 25% to a level of 40% over a period of three years."

Why to set goals at all ? Is it not enough if the objective alone is defined ? Research works done in this area suggest that goal-setting is essential. Many of us live and work far below our capacity. Psychologists tell us that most of us use only 10% of our capacities in any line. The research work done by Gary P. Latham & Garry A.Yukl. (Reference: "A review of research on the application of goal setting in organisations' - *Academy of Management Journal*, 1975) reveals the following.

a) Specific goals result in a higher level of performance than general goals or no goals at all.

[In the text book example quoted above, setting a specific goal of "increasing the market share from 25% to 40% over a period of three years" is expected to yield better results than the objective, or a general goal of "increasing the market share"]

b) Difficult/hard goals will result in higher performance than easy goals, provided the difficult goal is accepted as worthwhile and perceived to be attainable (whether or not it is ever actually attained).

Setting easily reachable goals serves no purpose. A goal set must be challenging. Just as a problem well defined is half solved, so a goal well set is half achieved. The very process of goal setting is found to develop a healthy tension within us that acts as a spur to accomplish them.

The crux of the problem lies in identifying what a challenging goal is. A manager, may, of course, find his subordinates claiming any goal as a challenging goal, however easily reachable they are!

But then, organisational objective should be achieved at any cost. Goals are a means to an end, viz., achieving organisational objectives. It is often noticed that even easier goals are achieved (or appear to be achieved !) only with great efforts.

The reasons are not hard to find. It is the under utilisation of human capacity as observed by the psychologists. Hence achieving organisational objectives will be within the easy reach of a chief executive if he ensures that goals are set at a slightly higher level than what is "normally considered adequate'. This will ensure that the employees come up with a little extra contribution (may be from 10% to 11% ?) for the achievement of goals and in turn for the fulfillment of organisational objectives

Thiruvalluvar had known the secret of setting higher goals for reaching organisational objectives.

> *"Higher and definite the goals aimed, easier are*
>
> *the objectives reached, surmounting hurdles on the way."*
>
> (Verse 596, *Thirukural*)

HUMILITY

Humility is the sense of recognising one's own several weaknesses and respecting other people's substantial strengths.

Managers who are under the notion that they know it all fail to be humble. Managers without humility do not listen to the views of others, never admit their mistakes, and are not interested in solving others' problems. They are interested only in their selfish ambitions and are prepared to even destroy others in their merciless mission to get to the top. Art is long, but life is short. One can not be master in all fields. *Thiruvalluvar* says that those who are stupid think that they know everything.

> *"It is nothing but stupidity if one thinks*
>
> *that he knows every thing."*

(Verse 844, *Thirukkural*)

A good manager will have all the humility to learn from others because he acknowledges that he does not have answers for all issues. By being humble, a manager does not appear belittled in the eyes of his colleagues and subordinates. On the contrary, he gains strength, credibility and respect.

> *"The great are always humble, while the mean*
>
> *will boast in self admiration."*

(Verse 978, *Thirukkural*)

Humility on the part of a manager not only helps in buildng up good interpersonal relationship with his team members, but also, according to *Thiruvalluvar*, helps to win over opponents.

> *"Humility will bring success; it will also be*
>
> *a wise man's weapon against his foes."*

(Verse 985, *Thirukkural*)

By being humble, a manger is endowed with the right mind-set to correctly judge the opponent's strengths and his own weaknesses. He is thus in a position carryout a more realistic SWOT analysis. When devoid of humility, a manager runs the risk of over-estimating his strengths and his opponent's weaknesses and under-estimating his weaknesses and his opponent's strengths and this may lead to ruin.

LEADERSHIP

"All managers manage, It is

leadership that makes the difference."

- McGregor.

Leadership is a process of influencing others in the group to act in a particular way in order to accomplish mutual goals. According to McFarland, leadership is ' the process of inter-personal influence by which the executive or manager influences the activities of others in choosing and attaining given ends."

Ordway Tead and Ervin Schell expounded the ' Trait theory ' of leadership, according to which an effective leader is one who possesses a combination of traits and qualities which enable him to influence others and get the work done through them. The common traits drawn by investigators and researchers were physical and nervous energy, a sense of purpose and direction, enthusiasm, friendliness and affection, integrity, technical mastry, decisiveness, intelligence, communication skill, empathy, self-confidence, foresight, etc.,

Studies were made at Ohio State University and Michigan University in America on leadership and the studies came out with the findings that the best way to study and define leadership is not to study the traits or qualities he possesses but to study his behaviour. This approach, called the 'behavioural approach' emphasises that what is important is not to know what a leader is but to study what he does or how he behaves in a particular situation.

Another approach to study leadership qualities by William Jenkins, Alvin Gourdner, Barrett, Fiedler etc., resulted in the formulation of 'Situation theory' of leadership. According to 'Situation theory', the leadership characteristics are a function of the specific situation. The success of a leader does not merely depend on the traits he possesses but on the particular situation at a time in which he exercises his leadership. It has been observed that a leader who is successful in one situation may not be successful in another situation.

All said and done, a leader moves with human beings. He gets things done through them. Hence, in order to be effective, he must win the confidence of his group members and subordinates. For winning their confidence, he must be open to their views and must be always prepared to accept his mistakes and correct his notions after an unbiased self analysis.

Alfred Tack observes on motivational leadership as under.

> "Being human beings it is very difficult for us to see our own faults, although we can always readily see faults in others.... Leaders must be

> open to reason - and being open to reason, must revise their own thinking if necessary...."

Dr. David Freemantle in his excellent work titled 'Super Boss' points out as under :

> "The more mistakes a manager admits, the more likely he or she is to be successful; manager gains strength from admitting mistakes and he also knows how to manage other people's mistakes. In admitting and managing mistakes, the manager facilitates remedial action and thus creates opportunities for improvement."

Let us see what *Thirukkural* has to say on the quality of a leader.

"He who corrects his own flaws first

before finding fault with others, is a good teacher."

(Verse 436, *Thirukkural*)

The quality of being open to the views of others, carrying out a self analysis and correcting his mistakes if any will stand the leader in good stead and his leadership will turn out to be effective.

What is the need for a leader in an organisation? Can an organisation which employs highly talented personnel achieve the objectives without a leader? The answer, obviously, will be an emphatic 'No'. The reason is not hard to find. It is the leader who builds a team combining the individuals, motivates the team and gives the team the direction to move towards achieving the organisational objectives. Putting it in other words, however strong and talented the employees are, if the leader is not an effective person. He cannot lead them to success. Thus, leader is the king pin of an organisation, and a manager must be a leader in the true sense of the word.

> *"Brave troops will become ineffective, in the absence of*
>
> *a commander leading them to success."*
>
> (Verse 770, *Thirukkural*)

For leading the team members to success, the leader must first gain their confidence. For the team members to have faith in their leader, *Thirukkural* advises that the leader must be fair and benevolent in his approach towards them.

> *"The world will praise those benign persons*
>
> *who are kind and benevolent."*
>
> (Verse 994, *Thirukkural*)

LEARNING

Learning is a never ending process. It starts in the womb and continues until death. Effective managers learn a little every day from their own mistakes, from the people who know more, from the specialists in functional disciplines, from the people on the job, in fact, virtually from everything that is surrounding them. They respect the knowledge, the experience, the skills and the wisdom of the people around them and draw from them valuable lessons. They never stop learning and never want to stop learning.

Thirukkural gives many advices on learning.

"Let a man learn flawlessly what is worthy to learn

and then stand firmly by what is learnt."

(Verse 391, *Thirukkural*)

Thirukkural advises one to learn "what is worthy to learn". A manager is expected to learn the right things and avoid the wrong things. Learning alone is not sufficient. One should act according to his learning.

Confucius has rightly said

> "The essence of knowledge is, having it, to use it."

Only learning is not enough; practising the good things learnt is of paramount importance.

> *"One who has learnt, advises others, but does not abide*
>
> *by what is learnt, is a fool no fool can equal."*
>
> (Verse 834, *Thirukkural*)

One should not stop learning. Managers who think that they know everything will definitely cause great damage to the organisation.

In the words of Dr. David Freemantle, "Once you stop learning you are dead, or at least you appear that way to your subordinates."

The more a manager learns, the greater will be his wisdom. One can refine and better his knowledge, as he keeps learning continuously. *Thirukkural* explains this with a simile as under.

> *"The more one learns, the fuller will be his knowledge*
>
> *just as the greater the water flows, the deeper a well is dug."*
>
> (Verse 396, *Thirukkural*)

Thus the gems of advices offered by *Thirukkural* that are useful for managers are:

"Learn what is worthy to learn;

practise what is learnt;

& Never stop learning, since the more you learn,

the fuller will be your knowledge."

LISTENING

Listening to the views of others is an art. This is an art more required of a manager. A manager must be a keen listener. He must be humble enough to know that he has much to learn from what others say. Another requirement of a good listener is to listen to the views of others without any bias or prejudice. When a person forms an opinion about another before start listening to his views, he builds a barrier that will prevent the ideas expressed by the other person to reach his mind. In fact the person receiving the message, may not be even aware that he has built a barrier around.

Jesus Christ often quotes in the new testament as under:

> "He that the hath ears to hear, let him hear' Jesus meant that there is more to understanding the message than merely the ability to hear. Listening means to pay attention, to concentrate, to use intelligence as well as ears and to perceive the meaning and significance of what has been heard.

Mere hearing does not make communication. Communication is effected only by listening. However, listening is not an easy thing to do. It needs a lot of understanding and practice.

People can think faster than they can talk or read. Hence unless the person who is receiving the message ' listens ' consciously to the speaker, there is a danger that his thoughts might tend to run ahead of the message and form opinions even before the message in fully received. Listening is a skill requiring great powers of stamina, self-control, concentration and understanding.

Managers who don't listen, especially when the subject does not suit their interest, are eager to interrupt, and interrupt without really listening to the views of the speaker. Such personalities are more frequently come across and they are sure to make ineffective managers.

'*Thirukkural* advises one to 'listen sharply'. It further adds to discern the truth after listening, *Thiruvalluvar* reaches a new height when he rightly advocates to listen the truth in everything by 'whomsoever' spoken, thereby he advises not to form any pre-conceived opinion before listening to the views of others. The words 'whomsoever' carries great relevance. A manager must be ready to listen to the views of all. The person who is offering a suggestion may be a junior in the organisation.

Even then, the manager must listen to his views as attentively as he would listen to the views of seniors / functional experts in the organisation. If does not matter if the manager rejects the views of juniors. They will be satisfied that their views are considered and analysed, and this feeling itself will be enough to improve their self confidence and self esteem. It would be still better, if the manager explains to them why their views were not accepted in a particular situation.

When a manager finds that the views of his subordinates differ from his views and accordingly decides not listen to the views of others, the message will go down very fast and people working under the manager may decide not to differ from the views of their boss. Thus, the manager may be deprived of some very valuable view points and various angles of approach to a problem.

"Those who enlighten their minds listening sharply will not speak foolishly even by slip of tongue."

(Verse 417, *Thirukkural*)

"To perceive clearly the truth in any matter spoken by anybody is wisdom."

(Verse 423, *Thirukkural*)

MIND DIVINING

When a person communicates with another person, he uses both verbal and non-verbal communication. Non-verbal messages are also called 'Silent messages.' Silent messages are those messages that people communicate through their facial expressions, tone of voice, gestures, appearance, posture and other non-verbal means. Research work done by Allan Pease (author of *'Signals, How to use body language for power, success and love'*) indicates that our non-verbal messages carry five times as much impact as verbal messages. This emphasises the importance of non-verbal communication. Allan Pease further concludes that about 7 per cent of our messages are conveyed through choice of words while 55 per cent are conveyed through facial expressions. Hence face acts as the index of the mind.

A manager, who is dealing with human beings throughout, has to be a good mind reader. He can not take for granted only the words of the mouth. He should have the ability to read the face of the communicator and to judge whether he really means what he says.

"As a mirror reflects what is in front

so the face reveals what is in the mind."

(Verse 706, *Thirukkural*)

When the body language, especially the facial expressions contradict the words, the manager must try to read the communicator's mind and understand the hidden message. This is a valuable skill that a manager should possess for him to be successful in judging the people around and to maintain good interpersonal relationships.

"He who reads the mind by look, without being told

will be an ornament to the world"

(Verse 701, *Thirukkural*)

Eyes transmit more message than any other part of the body. Hence, eyes act as windows through which a manager can look into the communicator's inner mind. Managers must develop the habit of establishing eye contacts when they give out or receive messages so that they can read the mind of the other person. This will be greatly improve the manager's understanding of the views and feelings of his subordinates, colleagues and even bosses.

"Those with subtle wisdom can be recognized

by observing their eyes that act as measuring instruments."

(Verse 710, *Thirukkural*)

PERSEVERANCE

Management is a process consisting of planning, organising, staffing, directing and controlling. All the above mentioned activities are aimed at achieving some thing that the enterprise desires to achieve. Thus, achievement is what management is all about. Results are the only measure of a manager's performance. The objective behind planning, organising, staffing, directing and controlling is to achieve the desired results. For achieving the desired results, the manager who is leading the team must have a strong committment and perseverance. The words of Swami Vivekananda — "Arise, Awake and stop not, till the goal is reached" — are not only applicable for religious pursuits, but are also suitable for business pursuits. The manager should not give up his efforts once he faces hurdles on his way. If the leader gives up his efforts, the team will only follow through. It is only in the hands of the leader to constantly motivate the team members, to lead them with perseverance towards the achievement of organisational objectives, however hard the path to achievement may be.

"What is aimed at is easier to achieve

when one pursues relentlessly with a firm mind."

(Verse 540, *Thirukkural*)

"There is nothing hard to achieve for those who persist

vigilantly with passion to achieve."

(Verse 537, *Thirukkural*)

The most difficult part of decision making is implementing the decision. A decision arrived at might be the right one. It might have been arrived at after analysing pros and cons. However, unless the decision is implemented properly, the whole exercise will become futile. Lack of will power to overcome any stumbling blocks on the way and absence of perseverance to fight till the end will only lead to dismal performance of the business enterprise.

"Perseverance will bring prosperity

and the lack of it will only breed poverty."

(Verse 616, *Thirukkural*)

"When a deed can lead to a happy end

pursue with firmness though hardships beset."

(Verse 669, *Thirukkural*)

Once a right course of action is chosen after due deliberations, the manager should not give up. There may be hurdles on the way. After all, the road to success will not be smooth. No pains no gains.

"The world will abandon those who give up

their tasks midway, unfinished."

(Verse 612, *Thirukkural*)

"Never give up saying, "It is had to achieve";

all pervasive efforts will overcome hurdles."

(Verse 611, *Thirukkural*)

During the course of implementing a decision, if the manager apprehends that the task ahead of him is hard to achieve, what should he opt to do? Even under such circumstances, Thiruvalluvar advises not to give up efforts. His words are consoling when he says that even if the task were to fail, the efforts taken would be paid for

"Even if fate acts against your mission, you will be

rewarded for your efforts."

(Verse 619, *Thirukkural*)

PERSONNEL SELECTION

Recruitment and selection of personnel is one of the vital areas of management. According to Edwin b. Fllippo, 'Recruitment is the process of searching for prospective employees and simulating them to apply for jobs in the organisation. Selection is the process of logically choosing individuals who possess the required skills, abilities and personality to successfully fill specific jobs in the organisation.

The success of an organisation significantly depends on the quality of personnel, which in turn depends on the effectiveness of selection process. A right person who is selected will be an asset to the organisation while the selection of a wrong person will mean an unwanted and unavoidable liability to the organisation for ever.

The success or failure of an organisation depends not on materials, machines and equipments, but on the efficiency of the personnel. In the words of Deyner, " Materials, machines and even offices themselves can be replaced and any risks involved can be insured against, but a good loyal team of workers can not be replaced so easily".

According to Dr. David Freemantle, "When you select the person, you select a potential contribution to profit". Any amount of time and effort is worth spending in the selection process since employees are the building blocks of the organisation.

Though selection is such an important function, it is not uncommon to find organisations selecting persons purely on the basis of recommendations (of political leaders, bureaucrats, union executives and other influential persons).

Almost all books on personnel management make a mention about selection of personnel based on recommendations as one the methods of selecting personnel. Loyalty to the organisation, economy, pre-disposition to accept the work environment etc., are also given as the supporting factors in favour of selection of personnel on the basis of recommendations. The harmful effects of such a policy will definitely be more serious in nature and will be detrimental to the interests of the organisation. Managers should not be carried away by the wrong notion that those selected on the basis of recommendations and influences would be personally loyal to them.

Thirukkural strongly advocates against selection of personnel based on influences and subjective considerations and advises managers to desist from giving consideration to personal loyalty in the selection process.

"To rely onpersonal loyalty to knowledge and
ability to perform is not the way to employ."

(Verse 515, *Thirukkural*)

There could be no compromise in the selection of personnel and the chief executive or the personnel manager who is in charge of the selection process should bear in mind that the organisation will flourish if selection of personnel is done on objective rather than subjective considerations and that the organisation will perish if subjective considerations and influences mar the selection process.

PERSONNEL WELFARE

In the words of Deyner, "materials, machines and even offices themselves can be replaced and any risks involved can be insured against, but a good loyal team of workers cannot be replaced so easily." Thus personnel management occupies a key position.

A war is won by the involvement of soldiers who fight in the fields. The Generals may provide plans and directions, but without the wholehearted contribution by the soldiers, victory is not possible. This is equally so in any business organisaton.

In the past, the industrialists and the managers believed that their only duty towards their employees was to pay them satisfactory wages. However, in the course of time, psychological researches proved that workers required something more important, i.e., human treatment. Understanding has now been reached that if the management of an organisation cares for its employees, the employees will take care of the organisaiton.

Hence the outlook of present day managers has changed from mere ' Profit through people ' to ' Profit through people, not at the expense of them.'

Work force are no longer considered as a mere 'Variable cost' as was considered in the past. On the contrary, work force is now being considered as a prized asset.

The present day personnel managers and HRD managers put forth their objectives as under.

- Workers should be provided with adequate remuneration.
- They should be provided with job security.
- They should be provided with increased job satisfaction.
- They should be given facilities for proper training & development.
- They should be provided with proper work environment.
- They should be provided with healthcare and recreational facilities.
- They should be provided with opportunities for advancement etc.

According to Peter F. Drucker, " the proper or improper use of the different factors of production depend of the wishes of the human resources. Hence, besides other resources, human resources need more development. Human resources can increase co-operation, but it needs proper and efficient management to guide it."

Though so much has been said about personnel

welfare, if we want to put it in one word, the manager should give top priority to the 'Interests' of the employees.

> *"Keep clear in mind the welfare of workers*
> *whose efforts depend the progress of the world."*
>
> (Verse 520, *Thirukkural*)

PLANNING

Management is the process of planning, organising, staffing, directing and controlling. Thus, planning is the first and foremost step in management. Putting it simply, planning is nothing but deciding in advance the future course of action. Let us see how planning has been defined by renounced management experts.

> 'To mastermind a management job, one must be able to plan effectively'. —J.M. Black
>
> 'Planning is an intellectual process, the conscious determination of course of action, the basing of decisions on purpose, facts and considered estimates'.
>
> —Koontz & Donnell
>
> 'Planning is fundamentally a mental disposition to do things orderly, to think before acting and to act in the right of facts rather than guesses'.
>
> —Lyndall Urwick
>
> 'Planning is the selection and relating of facts and making and using of assumptions regarding the future in the visualisation and

fomalisation of proposed activities believed necessary to achieve desired result.'

—G. Terry

Almost all the management experts are unanimous in their views on the importance of planning which can be summarised as under.

- Planning facilitates accomplishment of objectives.
- Planning ensures economy in operations.
- Planning provides for future contingency.
- Planning facilitates optimum utilisation of resources.
- Planning co-ordinates all activities.
- Planning provides for delegation of authority.
- Planning helps in reducing future risks and uncertainties.
- Planning facilitates control.

Let us see what *Thirukkural* says on planning.

"Exerting blindly without a definite plan ahead
is doomed to fail even if supported."

(Verse 468, *Thirukkural*)

Thirukkural gives a clear account of unplanned work. An unplanned endeavour is bound to fail and it can not be resurrected by any means whatsoever. This emphasizes the fact that efforts and investments, put in unplanned ventures are bound to go waste and any further effort / investment in support of rehabilitating and reviving such dying ventures will also go waste. It is something like trying to save a sinking ship in vain. Thus, Thirukkural brings out the importance of planning by pointing out the dire consequences of unplanned work.

PROACTION

Management must always foresee the future. Business enterprises can not be expected to react very quickly to unforeseen developments and take steps to encounter them. For example, a company does not (and can not) wait until its product becomes obsolete before coming up with a new product to replace the existing product. No enterprise can wait for problems to develop before preparing to face them. Proaction is an essential part of planning process.

Business cycle, for instance, is an important factor. Whether a business decision will be carried out in a period of boom or in a period of depression will make a lot of difference for its success. Strategic planning focuses an organisation's long term relationship to its external environment. Strategic planning focuses an organisation as a total system and recognizes that all enterprises face certain uncontrollable factors within their environment. The uncontrollable factors may be competitor's actions, changing economic scenario, regulatory mechanisms, shift in customer preferences etc., If an enterprise does not foresee the effects of such factors on its performance and take suitable counter measures, it will not only affect achievement of the enterprise's objectives, but will also do harm to its very survival.

Any enterprise, to survive continuously, must act proactively by resorting to appropriate strategic planning. In essence, strategic planning involves posing questions like the ones shown below and trying to arrive at answers to them.

a). What is our present business and what should it be ?

b). What business should we be in 5 years (or 10 years) from now ?

c). Who are our customers and who should our customers be?

d). Should we attempt to grow in the same business or opt to switch over to any other business ?

The answers to these questions will depend upon the strategic advantage or disadvantage that an enterprise has got. All firms have strategic advantages and disadvantages. But, unless a firm knows clearly as to what its strategic advantages are, it may not be in a position to choose the appropriate opportunity out of the opportunities available at a given time. So also, unless a firm analyses and finds out what its weaknesses are, it will not be prepared to meet and counter effectively any unanticipated environmental threats. *Thirukkural* advises proactive approach to guard against what it calls 'Surprise shocks'.

"Those who foresee and guard against evils are wise and will overcome surprise shocks."

(Verse 429, *Thirukkural*)

PROBLEM SOLVING

Of all the skills considered to be essential for managers, the most generally appreciated and emphasised are analytical skills and problem solving abilities. Every manager comes across problems and it is his responsibility to recognise, analyse and solve problems.

How do we define the term 'Problem' ? Any situation or circumstance that poses obstacles to achieving the organisational objectives can be considered to be a problem. Let us see how A. Leslie Derbyshire defines the term

'Problem', to have a broad idea about it.

> "We are constantly beset with circumstances that threaten to stop us from achieving our objectives, or at least to cause us serious delay. We get into situations that dissatisfy us and which we feel we must change. We ask - ' How can we change this loss situation into a profit situation ?' ' What can we do to eliminate these undesirable conditions ?' We may refer to these predicaments, dilemmas and emergencies as headaches, tough breaks or by other names, but

the general name that covers them all is Problems...."

According to Leavitt, problem solving skill represents almost the entire effort of many business schools. He estimates that about four-fifths of the MBA curriculum of top American schools is concerned with problem solving in one-way or another.

The methodology recommended by different management experts for solving problems are more or less the same Michel Armstrong enumerates the following steps as essential for problem solving.

- Define the situation
- Specify the objectives
- Develop hypothesis
- Get the facts
- Analyse the facts
- Consider possible courses of action
- Evaluate possible courses of action
- Decide and implement
- Monitor implementation.

The steps recommended by most of the management experts are stereotyped and are almost on the above lines.

Thirukkural gives a two-dimensional solution to problem solving.

"To do what should not be done and not to do what should be done are both ruinous."

(Verse 466, *Thirukkural*)

Thirukkural advises us not to do what should not be done and at the same time to do what should be done.

Quoting an instance, let a bank is faced with the problem of non-performing assets. The solution to tackle the problem of non-performing assets lies in attempting to improve the quality of asset portfolio from 'non-performing' to 'performing' one. It is not all that, The bank should at the same time concentrate in not adding to its portfolio, new assets that have potential to become 'non-performing' assets in the near future. Thus problem solving according to *Thirukkural* is a two-pronged approach of blocking the sources which create problems and attempting to solve the prevailing problems. Failure to block the sources that create problems and failure to attempt solving prevailing problems are both ruinous.

This underlines the need for tackling a problem from two directions for arriving at an effective solution. The wisdom of *Thirukkural* is sure to broaden the outlook of managers in solving problems.

PROJECT MANAGEMENT

Project Management has been evolved as a distinct discipline ever since the World War II. Though it has been practised ever since mankind started construction activities, it has got elevated as a special discipline only recently.

Project management consists of:

(a) Identifying the strategic place for locating the project.

(b) Arranging for the resources required to complete the project.

(c) Planning, scheduling and controlling the project 'implementation.

(d) Coordinating all the above activities by a properly formed project team.

Let us see what *Thiruvalluvar* says about project management. The entire gamut of Project management is given by *Thiruvalluvar* in the form of a capsule as under.

"Duly consider money, means, time, place and mode of execution, before proceeding with a task."

(Verse 675, *Thirukkural*)

Network techniques like CPM (Critical Path Method) and PERT (Programme Evaluation Review Technique) are being used in Project management for project planning and scheduling. Network planning & Scheduling techniques are useful in establishing precedence relationship between the activities of the project, in identifying the critical path, in studying the time-cost trade off relationship etc. Of these, identification of the critical path is an important aspect. Activities that lie on the critical path are the critical activities. Any delay in the completion of a critical activity will delay the project implementation time. Delayed project implementation may lead to cost over-run. The non critical activities [(i.e.) the activities that do not lie on the critical path] can be delayed, without increasing the overall completion time of the project. Thus critical activities require more attention in order to ensure that they are completed in time without any delay. Some amount of leniency can be allowed in respect of non critical activities. Their implementation can be delayed without increasing the overall project completion time and at the same time delaying the implementation of non-critical activities is likely to even reduce the project cost. The entire project scheduling technique revolves around identifying the activities that can be delayed and those that cannot be delayed and then suitably maneuvering the different activities to suit the time/cost constraints.

No one can be more precise and specific than *Thiruvalluvar* in giving guidance on scheduling of activities.

"Delay such acts than can be delayed

delay not acts that demand quick results"

(Verse 672, *Thirukkural*)

Project management calls for enormous skills, resources and acumen since it involves a complex set of activities to be performed. Hence unless a careful planning is done , the required resources are mobilised, and the project implementation is constantly monitored it is likely that the project may come to a grinding halt halfway through. There are many instances of projects getting delayed / stopped for want of resources and for want of skills on the part of the management. *Thiruvalluvar* cautions us not be over ambitious and not to take up projects that are beyond our means and reach.

"Those who do not assess their strength, but indulge in a task

fueled by ambition, invariably give up the task halfway through."

(Verse 473, *Thirukkural*)

"It is the peak of foolishness to aspire greedily

endeavours beyond ones capacity and reach."

(Verse 832, *Thirukkural*)

"Taking up tasks daringly, ignorant of their dimensions fools not only fail but also spoil the tasks, complicating them."

(Verse 836, *Thirukkural*)

PUBLIC SPEAKING

"Colleges teach the one thing that is perhaps the most valuable for future employee to know. But, very few students bother to learn it. This one basic skill is the ability to organise and express ideas in writing and speaking. As soon as you move one step from the bottom, your effectiveness depends on your ability to reach others though the spoken or written words. And the farther away your job is from manual work, the larger the organisation of which you are an employee, the more important it will be that you know how to convey your thoughts in writing or speaking. In the very large organisation, this ability to express oneself is perhaps the most important of all the skills a person can posses".

—Peter F. Drucker

The words of Peter F. Drucker brings out the importance of 'Public speaking' skills that a manager should possess.

Thiruvalluvar puts in two verses the importance of skills of expression, more effectively as under.

"The learned who are unable to express

are flowers without fragrance."

(Verse 650, *Thirukkural*)

"What use of swards to cowards or learning to the learned

fearful of an intelligent assembly ?."

(Verse 726, *Thirukkural*)

The success of a speaker lies in knowing the audience. The speaker should know in advance the personal characteristics of the audience, such as, their age, sex, education, experience, knowledge of the subject matter etc. The more the speaker knows about the audience, the better he could adapt his presentation to suit the audience.

"Those who speak unavailingly without knowing their audience

though speak at length, are poor orators."

(Verse 713, *Thirukkural*)

Effective leaders use words that have the same meaning for both speakers and listeners. Use of complicated words and complex sentences with a view to impressing the audience rather than expressing the ideas are of no avail. In fact, simple words and short sentences simplify complex ideas.

"Delivering effective speech choosing flawless words

is the sign of scholarly mind."

(Verse 717, *Thirukkural*)

The speaker must be capable of capturing the attention of the audience. He should speak at natural volume and in a natural tone. He should use variation in volume of his speech for emphasising important subject matter. A good speaker should use eye contacts and gestures to bind the attention of his audience.

Thirukkural emphasises the need for effectiveness in delivering speech, by saying that the speaker should attract even those who are disinterested in the subject matter.

"A speech is outstanding if it binds the audience

and attracts the opposed and disinterested as well."

(Verse 643, *Thirukkural*)

During feedback/discussion sessions at the end of a presentation, if any of the audience expresses views different from that of the speaker, until shown otherwise, the speaker should assume that the other party has some reasonably good reasons for the position he/she has taken. A good speaker shall not attack the conclusions of his opponent. He shall only attack the reasoning that took the opponent to his conclusion.

Directly disagreeing with the conclusion mostly does not produce the expected result. To get the opponent alter his opinion, the speaker has got to erode the foundations upon which the opponent's conclusions are built.

> *"Learn the rule of logic so that you may, in an assembly,*
>
> *counter without fear and convince by arguments."*
>
> (Verse 725, *Thirukkural*)

REPRIMANDING

There is no denying the fact that a manager must use sweet words, especially with his subordinates. There is also no second opinion that a manager must not fail to praise his subordinates when they do anything good. This is because, when a manager praises his subordinates, they feel good about themselves. This is more so when they are praised in public and that too in front of their colleagues. This motivates others also to perform better. Human beings at all levels enjoy occasional pats on the back ('Strokes' as transactional analysts call them).

Effective management does not mean praising and praising alone. It also includes reprimanding. If a manager ignores some mistake committed by his employees, if he fails to correct poor performance of some others, it will encourage negligence and promote casual attitude in work. This will be most undesirable and counter-productive in nature. The secret of a successful manager lies not only in praising his subordinates for their good acts but also in reprimanding them for the lapses on their part.

A manager is expected to practise a balanced blend

of giving positive and negative feed backs in the right place and in the right measure.

While reprimanding a person for his lapse, a manager must be very careful in his attitude and he must ensure that he is perceived as critising only the wrongful act and not the person. The manager should make it clear that there is nothing wrong about the person as an employee and that he still holds him in the same high esteem as an individual.

Most important of all, reprimand should be done strictly in private and not in public. It must also be very brief. A right reprimand can mend a person while a wrong reprimand will injure his feelings and may even kill the good worker in him.

Thirukkural has a lot to tell us on this issue.

Thiruvalluvar says in clear terms that harsh words may be used when needed. But he is very particular in ensuring that any reprimand should be brief and without being a noisy affair.

"Harsh words may be used, as need be, but let not

men of worth use in vain futile words."

(Verse 197, *Thirukkural*)

The words 'as need be ' in the above verse require careful observation. In another verse given below, *Thiruvalluvar* advises to use sweet words wherever it suits. Hence it can be inferred that the advice from *Thirukkural* is to use harsh words only as a last resort.

"Speaking harsh words when sweet words suit

is like choosing raw fruits when ripe fruits exist."

(Verse 100, *Thirukkural*)

The words ' when sweet words suit' convey the advice to use sweet words even for reprimand if they suit. This is a refinement in thought and will go a long way in establishing better interpersonal relationship and better organisational efficiency.

Thiruvalluvar goes one step further and advocates another technique when he says to put the evil doer to shame by doing him good.

"The (proper) punishment of those who have done evil

is to put them to shame by showing kindness to them."

(Verse 314, *Thirukkural*)

This will be the most effective way to make a person realise his fault, to repent for his lapse and to make a resolve not to commit the fault ever again.

RISK TAKING

Risk, in financial management, is associated with the variability of the rates of return from an investment. The most fundamental tenet of finance literature is that there is a trade off between risk and return. The risk-return relationship requires that the return on an investment should commensurate with its riskiness. There is always an investment that does not involve any risk. Such risk free investments offer a very lower rate of return on the investment. When an investor is afford to bear some amount of risk, he can go for riskier investments. Higher the risk perception of an investment proposal, higher the return. Since more risky investments offer higher returns, it does not imply than an investor can choose that investment which offers the maximum return. Such an investment will be having the maximum risk which the investor may not be able to withstand.

The risk bearing capacity of investors vary according to their financial strength. However, even if an investor is financially strong enough and can venture to choose that investment which is the most risky, it is not advisable for one to do that. The development of modern portfolio theory is based on the principle of diversifying the investment in order to reduce the risk level of the portfolio of investments.

Thirvalluvar advises not to invest in high risk ventures since, according to him the high gains expected from such high risk ventures are ' doubtful ' in nature. By the word ' doubtful ' he means a higher variability of return, i.e., it can either offer a very high return or the return may be unexpectedly low, if conditions turnout to be unfavourable.

"The wise never risk their capital, anticipating

doubtful gains and lose their all."

(Verse 463, *Thirukkural*)

Even if one gets a very high return from a very risky investment, it only means that the statistics of probability has worked in his favour and there is no guarantee that the same risky investment will offer the same high return the second time.

"Abstain from gambling even if you have won;

your gain is only a bait in a trap to draw you in."

(Verse 931, *Thirukkural*)

When economic/business conditions are fluctuating and uncertain, enterprises that have a larger proportion of debt as compared to equity capital are exposed to the risk of becoming unable to repay their debt obligations. Though it is not necessary to shun debt altogether, it must be ensured that the debt-equity ratio should be such that under any eventuality debt repaying capacity of the enterprise will not get affected.

Thiruvalluvar outlines the safety involved in running an enterprise with sufficient wealth. The words 'sufficient wealth' only indicates that the proportion of debt to equity should be one that the enterprise can afford to bear under any worst conditions. *Thiruvalluvar* explains this with the help of a simile.

"Venturing on a task with sufficient wealth in hand

is as safe as viewing an elephant-fight from a hill-top."

(Verse 758, *Thirukkural*)

Another subtle message is hidden behind the words ' sufficient wealth in hand'. An enterprise might have been started with a higher proportion of debt. Even then, if the enterprise has other forms of sufficient wealth/assets to fall back upon in the event of unforeseen losses etc., the enterprise will be safe and will be able face troubled times with ease. One who is watching an elephants fight from the top of a hill will remain unaffected however fierce the fight may be. Similarly one who has ventured to start an enterprise with sufficient wealth in hand will remain unaffected even when the business climate turns worse.

SOCIAL RESPONSIBILITY OF BUSINESS

The concept of social responsibility of business has been discussed for about a century. Though there was a section of thought that did not favour including social responsibility in business considerations, the concept has been gradually gaining recognition and a stage has come that social responsibility has been accepted as an essential responsibility of business.

Of late, we come across many instances of business houses undertaking social activities, like, BHEL contributing to adult education, Escorts Ltd., working for form mechanisation, agricultural development and healthcare, ITC Ltd., undertaking pollution control activities, TISCO resorting to community development and tribal area development etc.,

Koontz & Donnell defined social responsibility as "...the personal obligation of the people as they act in their own interests, to assume that the rights and legitimate interests are not impinged. . . ." The definition by Koontz & Donnell gives a only passive dimension to the concept of social responsibility.

H.R. Bowen observes that social responsibility is

"...the obligation (of managers) to pursue those policies to make those decisions or to follow those lines of action which are desirable in terms of the objectives and values of our society...." Though Bowen has improved upon the scope of social responsibility, there is still something more to be desired.

Social responsibility is the bounden duty of business because it is the society that supports business. Business does not exist in vacuum. On the face of it, there are many to whom the business is definitely responsible, viz., the share holders, the employees, the suppliers, the creditors, the customers, the Government etc. These apart, the business is very much responsible for the society that sustains its existence. Though the shareholders, the employers, the suppliers, the creditors, the customers, the Government etc., are visible for the part that they play, the society's role for the sustenance of business is not apparently visible. It is hidden underneath like the foundation that lies under the building.

Business can recognise its responsibility to the society only if it realises that social responsibility in its 'duty.'

Thiruvalluvar gives an immortal definition of 'duty.'

"Duty seeks nothing in turn as rain seeks not compensation;

Can the world recompense rain for what it has received?."

(Verse 211, *Thirukkural*)

The rain supports the world on its own, without anticipating any thing in return. The world that receives the gifts of rain and that subsists only because of rain cannot compensate the rain. The society supports the business and hence it is the bounden duty of the business to support the society without anticipating anything in return.

Once the business gets the insight of its duty to the society that supports it, it can not remain without being socially responsible.

STAFFING

Staffing is one of the major functions of management. Staffing function deals with human beings of different backgrounds, skills, interests and personal traits.

Staffing function concerns the recruitment, selection, training and development of personnel, and assigning the right jobs for the right persons. Good staffing ensures effective performance of other functions as well and hence better results. Staffing functions thus helps in building a sound pool of human resources with perfect matching of their abilities with the requirements.

Dr. A.S. Ganguly, who was chairman of Hindustan Lever Ltd., (1980-1990) observed as under:

> "...By a combination of factors, Hindustan Lever was able to attract a group of ordinary people and enable them to perform extraordinarily...."

A close observation of his statement will bring out the fact that it was the effective staffing that has enabled ordinary people perform extraordinarily.

In fact there is no group of people who can be termed 'Ordinary'. Every individual has inherent abilities to perform certain jobs better than others. The success of staffing function depends on identifying the capability of individuals, nurturing their talents in their respective areas of interest and providing them with job opportunities matching their skills. Once such a perfect harmony is achieved, success will be pre-written story.

Thus, staffing function helps in making best case of the talents of persons working in the organisation and enables them to use their potential for the betterment of the organisation. This apart, staffing function also helps individuals in achieving their individual personal gains, which also goes a long way in enhancing their performance and contribution to the organisation.

The concept of 'right man for the right job' has been brought out by *Thirukkural* in simple terms.

"Select a person with qualities required to accomplish the kind of job and then entrust the job to him."

(Verse 517, *Thirukkural*)

STRESS MANAGEMENT

Stress is a state of tension experienced by individuals facing extraordinary demands, constraints or opportunities. All executives undergo stress. Some handle it well, other handle it poorly. Stress affects the health of an individual. It is a potential source of both anxiety and frustration, each of which, in turn, is capable of breaking down the body's physiological and / or psychological well being over time.

Stress has been found to be the major cause of disease like heart attacks, strokes, bronchitis etc., and a cause of ineffectiveness in managers.

The factors that cause stress, called stressors are divided into three categories, as under.

a) Work factors [Task demands, Role dynamics, Interpersonal relationships and career progress]

b) Personal factors [Needs, Capabilities and Personality]

c) Network factors [Family, Economics & Personal affairs]

of all the factors, disruption of normal home life (which comes under network factors) like death, divorce, separation etc., have been found to be the major contributors of stress. Present day executives are more stressed personalities as compared to their counterparts of yester years. Executives of the future are going to be more stressed personalities than the present day executives.

Many stress management techniques have been advocated by management thinkers and psychologists of which 'mental relaxation' is one of the important techniques.

Mental relaxation is a skill that is rarely taught, though it is the main tool for stress management. Though many books set out relaxation techniques, nothing is of real help to executives to relieve stress. In fact those who know how to relax never need to know how they do it and those who do not know how to relax will never learn from the so called relaxation techniques.

Relaxing the mind is a secret. It is one that can be achieved instantaneously, if one has got the correct outlook of life. At the same, it is one that can never be achieved, however hard one tries, if his outlook of life is not correct. Relaxation is a state of mind that will prevail if one has the correct insight into life.

Thirukkural is full of philosophical ideas which help one to view the world in the right perspective.

> *"Life is a game, pain and sorrow are parts of it;*
>
> *the wise are not unduly bothered."*

(Verse 627, *Thirukkural*)

Stress is the result of worries. Worries are caused due to pain and suffering, either physical or mental. *Thiruvalluvar* depicts a clear picture stating that pain and suffering are part of the game of life. There is no undoing it. It has to be accepted as it is. Hence the wise are not worried about it as there is no meaning in worrying.

"Confused mind deems trivial things worthy

and makes life miserable and meaningless."

(Verse 351, *Thirukkural*)

Worries are the result of considering trivial things worthy and vice versa. This makes our lives miserable. But then, how to know what trivial things are. The answer lies in the following verse.

"Misjudging fleeting things as lasting ones

is the worst of follies in life."

(Verse 331, *Thirukkural*)

Fleeting things are trivial. Judging by this scale, everything about which a person worries will all be fleeting things. The manager might be finding it difficult to manage the labour unrest in his organisation, his boss might rebuke him for no fault of him, his family life might be a failure. But these are all not lasting ones as *Thiruvalluvar* puts it. He says that it is foolish to worry misjudging such fleeting things as lasting things.

Thiruvalluvar goes on to guide us as to how to be free from worries. He reiterates the wisdom of many saints that desire is the root cause of all troubles.

"Destroy desires, the most painful of pains

to enjoy happiness for ever."

(Verse 369, *Thirukkural*)

And finally *Thiruvalluvar* unveils the secret formula of destiny and disposition of God.

"What is more powerful than fate.? Its will

will overcome human skill."

(Verse 380, *Thirukkural*)

"Any extent of wealth amassed may not be enjoyed

except as proposed by the Great Disposer."

(Verse 377, *Thirukkural*)

Indian philosophy relies strongly on fate and the supremacy of God, the Great Disposer. When one accepts that all are the acts of the Great Disposer, one will not get unduly disturbed by anything that happens in his life. This is the mental disposition that *Thiruvalluvar* wants to inculcate in the minds of all. By accepting such a stand, it does not mean that a manager will become less efficient. On the contrary he will become more efficient in performing his duties and virtues that are desired in a manager, like. Humility, Compassion, Honesty, Integrity, Impartiality etc., will descend on him. He will be a person bubbling with enthusiasm and activities, but at the same time calm and serene inside. He will be always in a state of mental relaxation and will never be prone to stress.

TIMELY ACTION

Out of the three resources of money, time and people, time is a unique resource. One cannot rent, hire, buy or otherwise obtain more time. Hence, time once lost is lost forever.

Organisational decisions can be broadly classified into two categories, viz., programmed decisions and non-programmed decisions. Identifying and understanding the problem, developing alternative solutions for the problem, and evaluating the different courses of action are the steps followed for making programmed decisions. Considerable research work has been done on programmed decision making. However, non-programmed decision making, which is also a situation frequently faced by top executives and which is more prone to delays has somehow escaped serious attention.

Higher level executives are often required to make non-programmed decisions, where each time a new situation is encountered and each new situation demands a new decision depending upon the specific nature of the situation. An executive who is up against a situation in which he is under compulsion to make a non-programmed decision, must act swiftly.

Such situations demand a high level of self confidence, courage, conviction and also the ability to store, sift and analyse information relevant to the given decision making situation. All this must be done fast, without any delay since invariably non-programmed decision situations need immediate action.

Most executives face non-programmed decision situations with unease since they fear the adverse consequences of their decisions , in the event of their decisions turning out to be wrong. This makes most of the executives to follow the line of least resistance and take 'safe' decisions irrespective of whether such decisions are in tune with the organisational interests or not. They resort to 'safe' decisions in order to safeguard their own personal interests, even if such decisions are detrimental to the overall interests of the organisation. It is more likely that such over cautious, safe, defensive decisions are always delayed decisions.

When an executive who is to make a non-programmed decision prefers to take a 'safe' path, he will be missing the rare opportunities that may exist in such decision situations.

The opportunity available in a non-programmed decision situation may be one of taking advantage of the existing favourable conditions for the benefit of the organisation or one of safeguarding against unfavourable conditions to avoid harmful consequences. Once missed, opportunities rarely reappear. Especially when the future is gloomy, making non programmed decisions require certain amount of boldness and self confidence on the part of the decision maker. He should look for the hidden opportunities, analyse the situation swiftly and take a decision that is rational, remunerative, effective, reasonable and that serves the interests of the organisation rather than delaying the process and taking a 'safe' decision which is not in the organisational interest.

> *"When a rare opportunity comes, do not hesitate while it lasts;*
>
> *swiftly accomplish tasks that will otherwise remain unaccomplished."*
>
> (Verse 489, *Thirukkural)*

TRUST

Trust is the essence of all meaningful relations, whether at home or at workplace or anywhere else. A successful manager will always have implicit trust in his team and his team will have trust in him. Trust is the emotional bond that binds leaders and followers together. Trust is the essential ingredient of any organisation. It is said to be the lubricant that maintains the organisation friction-free. In a climate of distrust, politics flourish and much energy is wasted in protecting one's own interest, in damaging others interests/reputation. Distrust, thus acts counter-productive and generates hostile industrial relationships.

An effective manager must develop trust by devoting enough time to building honest relationships with his people. He will not blindly trust his people. He will test before trusting. What are the aspects that need to be considered while studying/testing a person to asertain if he is trustworthy? *Thirukkural* gives us the required guidance.

"Noble heritage, devoid of vices and shame of faults

are norms to rely on, to choose the worthy."

(Verse 502, *Thirukkural*)

Without putting a person to test, a manager is not expected to repose his trust on him. But, once he has reposed his trust on a person after due test and trail, he should not give room for distrust, which will only spoil the interpersonal relationship and the confidence of the subordinates on their boss.

"Trust no one without testing; after testing

assign work that suits one."

(Verse 509, *Thirukkural*)

"Reposing trust before testing and entertaining distrust

after trusting are both harmful."

(Verse 510, *Thirukkural*)

While *Thiruvalluvar* advises not to trust any one untried, he cautions that reposing trust without test and suspecting after reposing trust are both harmful. By this *Thiruvalluvar* only means that effective manager should always give others the benefit of the doubt and never believes 'evil' of them unless clear evidence is found.

When trust level is an organisation is high, employees express faith and confidence in the leadership. Without trust, people fear revealing their thoughts and feelings. If the level of trust is low, people tend to raise their defences and communication suffers.

Just as a leader should try and trust his subordinates, he should be one in whom his subordinates repose trust. When people trust their leader, they function naturally and openly. Without trust, they divert their energies to hide their true feelings and views.

What are the qualities that a leader should have so that his subordinates will repose trust in him? Thiruvalluvar readily comes with an answer.

> *"The pillars of goodness are five - love, fear of sin*
>
> *benevolence, compassion and truthfulness."*

(Verse 983, *Thirukkural*)

INDEX

□□□